ROCKS AND MINERALS OF THE WORLD

Speedy Publishing LLC

40 E. Main St. #1156

Newark, DE 19711

www.speedypublishing.com

All rocks are made of
two or more minerals,
but minerals are not
made of rocks.

Granite is an igneous rock. Granite is one of the hardest substances in the world. Granite is considered the most abundant basement rock on the Earth.

Granite has been extensively used as a dimension stone and as flooring tiles in public and commercial buildings and monuments.

Limestone is
a sedimentary
rock. Limestone
can most
abundantly be
found in the
shallow ends of
marine water.

Limestone is often used
in construction such as
being added to paint
as a thickening agent.

Marble is a metamorphic rock. Marble usually lays among the oldest part of the Earth's crust.

Marble is used as an artful rock. The stone is particularly popular among sculptors especially the white varieties.

11
80.1
2(β⁻, γ) 20
B
Bor
26.981
27
100
26(β⁺, γ) 7.2·10
5.9
Al

Aluminum is a silvery-white, soft, nonmagnetic, ductile metal. It is the most abundant metal found naturally on Earth.

Aluminum is globally the most used metal that does not contain iron. One of the most popular uses of aluminum is packaging.

Gold is shiny, soft and dense. Gold is the most malleable of all metals. It can easily be beaten into thin sheets or other shapes.

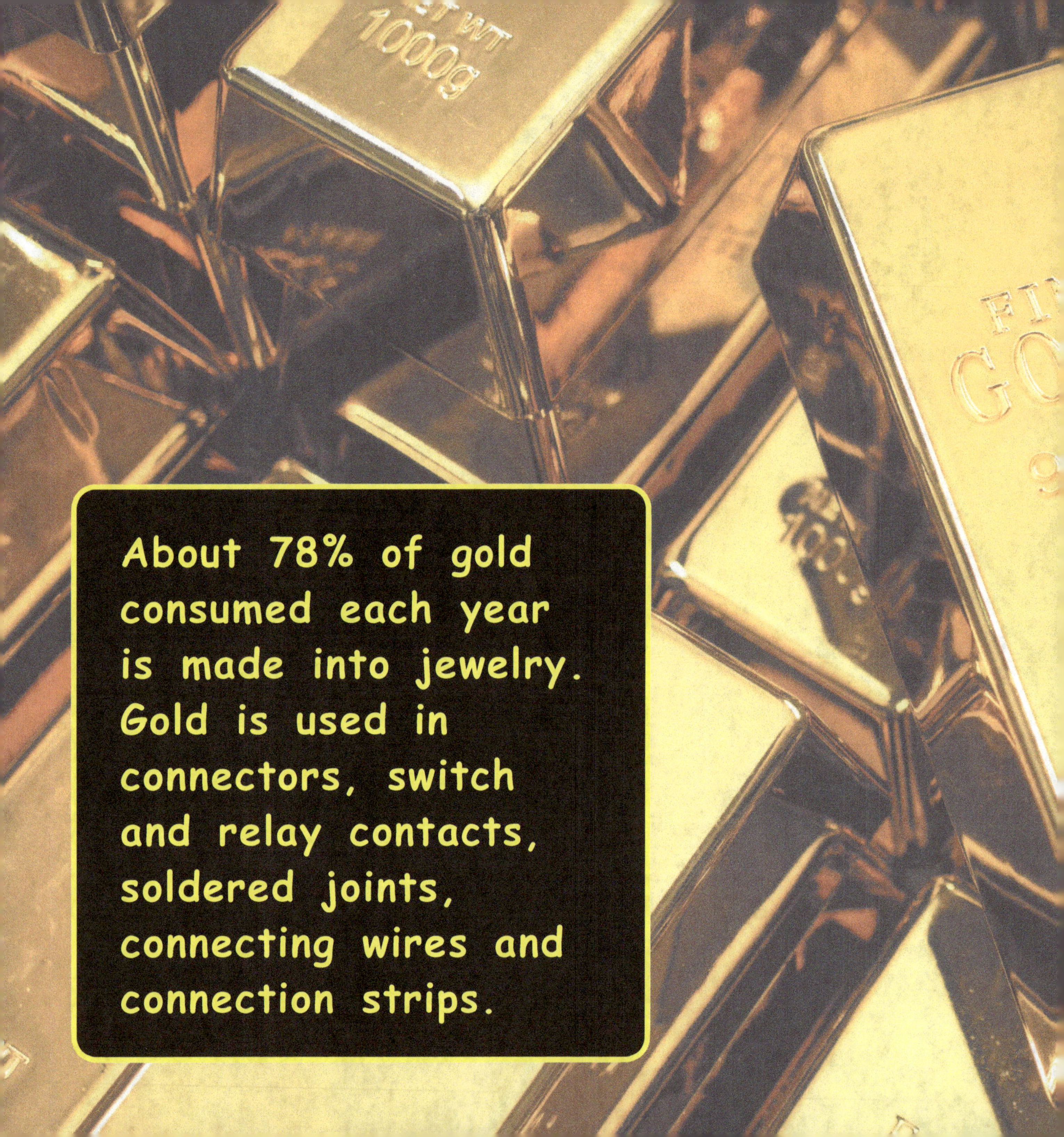
About 78% of gold consumed each year is made into jewelry. Gold is used in connectors, switch and relay contacts, soldered joints, connecting wires and connection strips.

FINE
GOLD
999.9
NET WT
1000g
FINE
GOLD
999.9
NET WT
1000g
FINE
GOLD
999.9

Silver has the highest electrical conductivity of all the elements. Silver was one of the first metals discovered by ancient peoples.

Silver is precious metal that
has been used for many
years to make fine pieces of
jewelry, coins and utensils.

Diamond is
the hardest
mineral in
nature.
Most of
the Earth's
natural
diamond
deposits
are found
in Africa.

Diamonds are used to make jewelry. It is also used to cut, grind and bore into other hard materials.